PROPHET Come out *of your* Cave

MICHAEL BACON

CONTENTS

FOREWORD

Michael Bacon's book, Prophet Come Out Of Your Cave, is a very timely book. It is a book that I totally recommend for the Body of Christ, especially those involved in the five-fold ministry or in intercession. I would encourage you to read with spiritual ears and eyes and not from a denominational filter. I believe this book will awaken hearts to move from the old wineskin to a new wineskin. Whenever you have a move of the Holy Spirit, you will always have counterfeits appear; but God is raising up His true tribe that will be taught, trained and released. Michael Bacon has a heart for the body of Christ to be transformed and renewed in wisdom and revelation.

Rev. Solomon J. Buckley
Overseer / Director: Fresh Wind International Missions Base Inc.

BIO

Michael Bacon is the husband of Lyn Bacon, father of eight children, and grandfather of seven. Michael is Apostle and Co-Founder of Freedom Life Church (FLC) in Angier, North Carolina. He has a Master's in Christian Leadership from Liberty University and has been in ministry since 2007. He believes in the Body of Christ fulfilling the work of God and fully endorses mentorship, discipleship, as well as equipping, activating and releasing people into the ministry. The Lord has commissioned him to raise up five-fold ministers that can reach the world for Christ. He has also done missions work in Nigeria and experienced many healing miracles in his ministry. His main gifts to the body of Christ are in prophecy, exhortation and healing. Michael is available for speaking engagements and revivals throughout the world. To contact him you may email him directly at Michael.t.bacon@gmail.com.

DEDICATION

This book is dedicated to my lovely wife Lyn and our beautiful children and grandchildren.

INTRODUCTION

The Bible tells us that there will be an outpouring of the Holy Spirit that will come upon all flesh in the last days before Jesus returns. This is prophesied in the second chapter of Joel, and then again in second chapter of Acts. "Acts 2:17-21 – And it shall come to pass in the last days, saith God, I will pour out of my Spirit upon all flesh; and your sons and daughters shall prophesy, and your young men shall see visions, and your old men shall dream dreams; And on my servants and on my handmaidens I will pour out in those days of my Spirit, and they shall prophesy; And I will show wonders in Heaven above, and signs in the earth beneath; blood, and fire, and vapor of smoke; The sun shall be turned into darkness, and the moon into blood, before that great and noteable day of the Lord come; And it shall come to pass, that whosoever shall call on the name of the Lord shall be saved."

During this end-time outpouring, we will see many things happen on the earth. The Bible tells us that we can expect earthquakes, volcanoes, wars, rumors of wars, famines and floods. Many people in the world will become fearful as these prophecies unfold. Evil will grow so strong that people will begin to do the unthinkable. Murders, rapes, torture, sexual perversity and many other sinful acts will become ordinary behaviors as the world is given over to a reprobate mind. People will wonder if there is any safety as crime will invade even the richest neighborhoods. Status, class, or wealth will not protect people, as the days grow more and more dark. This time is prophesied in the Bible when Jesus told His disciples that it would be just as the days of Noah when He returned. "Luke 17:26 – "And as it was in the days of Noe, so shall it be also in the days of the Son of man."

During the days of Noah, we know that God was very upset because there was so much evil everywhere. The Lord was so disgusted with the sinful state of man that He decided to flood the earth and kill all its inhabitants with the exception of Noah's family. Noah's family were the only people spared, but afterwards God made a covenant with man represented by a rainbow in the sky whereby the Lord promised the world that He would never flood it again. However, the Bible clearly indicates that the last days before Jesus returns will be just as evil as the days of Noah. It is all part of God's plan before His great return.

In preparation for the final days, we will see a major shift in the church. People will no longer be satisfied with religion, tradition, or church as usual. There will be a great conviction, hunger and a thirst for more of God. A revival of great proportions will begin in the church. People we thought were saved will reveal their true hearts, and those that we thought were lost will find Jesus. There will be multitudes that give their hearts to the Lord in this hour. As part of this move of God we will see apostles and prophets raised up to bring a true five-fold ministry back to the church. The people that God will raise up in this hour will not be people who are seeking titles or chasing positions in the church. It will be those we least expect who have been broken and tested before God. Satan will even know who these people are and will target them from childbirth forward. There will also be a changing of the guard as God removes some and raises up others.

The Bible says that many are called but only few are chosen. During the days ahead we will see a rebuilding of the five-fold ministry in the church. There is a need for more apostles and prophets to be raised up in the church today. This book will focus on those that are called to the office of prophet. There are many that God is raising up for this very important office. If the nations ever needed to hear God it is certainly now. For those of you that God is raising up as prophets, it will not be an easy walk. Satan's mission in the last days is not to simply spread evil, but also to destroy God's prophets. If you are called to be a prophet, you will have to pay a price for the anointing that you will carry. The enemy will viciously attack every person who is called to the prophetic office. I have come to understand that, in the life of a prophet, we should expect attacks to happen in our lives. We shouldn't wonder if we are going to be attacked, because it is clear that we can expect the attacks to come. It is not a matter of *if*, but of *when* the attacks will come. If you are called as a prophet, the attacks will come. Expect them and be ready for them.

As prophets we have to be ready for battle at a moment's notice. We have to cleanse our lives of things that are displeasing to God. In preparation for this battle, the Lord will often work within the heart of a prophet to weed out the things that are not of Him. God deals with each prophet according to the heart and is exposing every area of weakness that could bring sin, disobedience, or a spirit of fear. I have talked to many prophets in my lifetime and they have all told me the same thing. They each felt that they had a target on their back. They could literally feel that someone or something was against them. Many prophets are weary and frustrated with God because the attacks and battles are so fierce that they often feel abandoned and alone. These prophets often flee the presence of God to enter a cave of self-pity and discouragement just as Elijah did when Jezebel threatened to kill him. The enemy's strategy is quite clear: hunt down and destroy the prophets of God. That is why I believe we are seeing an increase in abortions today. Satan is literally killing God's prophets before they are even born.

Satan and his demons will use any weapon they can get their hands on to discourage, stop, or even destroy the prophet. If he cannot stop the prophet from doing God's work, he will even resort to setting the prophet up to fall into sin or discredit their ministry somehow. He often uses offenses, rejection, abandonment, threats, misunderstandings and divisions to destroy the prophet. In fact, one of Satan's greatest strategies is to get God's prophets to leave the local church to go out on their own. Once the prophet removes himself/herself from the local body, they become an easy target for the enemy to destroy. Once removed from accountability and the local body, the prophet no longer has a covering or protection. This can lead to their destruction. Many of these prophets who leave the local church become very discouraged and go into a cave of self-pity or depression. Some never make it back to ministry to fulfill the will of God.

God is calling the prophets out of their caves. He is calling His prophets to take their positions. This is part of the great out-pouring that was mentioned in the second chapter of Acts. The Lord is releasing a greater anointing in this hour similar to what Elijah and Elisha walked in. Like Elijah, we cannot let the world and people in the world intimidate or discourage us. We must stay in right relationship with the Lord and understand the anointing and authority that we walk in. Isaiah 54:17 says, "No weapon that is formed against thee shall prosper; and every tongue that shall rise against thee in judgment thou shalt condemn. This is the heritage of the servants of the Lord, and their righteousness is of me, saith the Lord."

Until Elijah's encounter with Jezebel, he walked in more power than almost any other prophet had walked in before. He called down fire from the heavens, raised the dead, healed the sick, and defeated the false prophets of Baal. There was no one that could stop him because God Himself was with Elijah. Whatever Elijah spoke came to pass. In the first chapter of 2 Kings, we read about Elijah calling down the fire of God that destroyed the armies and in the eighteenth chapter of 1 Kings, we read how Elijah was able to call down the fire of God and then had authority to kill all the prophets of Baal. Yet, later we read that Elijah's life was threatened by Jezebel; and, instead of standing against her, he ran for his life and hid in a cave. How can a man of God who moved in such power now find himself in a cave hiding from one woman? In answering this question, we will find the answers that prophets need in order to move forward into their destiny and purpose.

CHAPTER 1

Are You Called to be a Prophet?

In the last ten to twenty years, we see many people who are now calling themselves "apostles" and "prophets." These days, there are new apostles and prophets popping up every day. With many people claiming to be apostles and prophets, why are we not seeing more miracles, signs, and wonders? The reality is that many people are not seeking God or the will of God, but instead are seeking a position or a title to be elevated before others. Those that take on these titles without them being given by God are walking in a dangerous place as the Lord holds each person accountable to the title they walk. With the title comes great responsibility and accountability to the Lord. God has ordained each person for a purpose. To take on any other purpose other than what God intended for us will only delay our blessings and bring destruction to our lives. We must surrender to what God has called us to and not to something that was never ours. It is important that each person discovers their calling and purpose and begins to walk it out as soon as possible in order to fulfill the destiny that God intended. The time in this world is truly short. We should be careful not to waste even a day of it.

Many people in the body of Christ are going nowhere in their ministries, because they have assumed titles, positions, and ministries to which God never called them. Many are outside the will of God and are not in position to advance the kingdom of God in this hour. Because of this, we are seeing a real delay in the spiritual outpouring that the Lord wants to release to the earth. The church is solely responsible for this delay. We keep on waiting for God to show up, but God is waiting for His people to get into position. The sooner that the church lines up with the word of God and gets in position, the sooner we can see the greatest outpouring this world has ever seen.

As part of this outpouring, there are specific people that God is calling to the office of prophet. God chooses people for this office that He has designed to walk in His authority and as His mouthpiece upon the earth. He has predestined these prophets to usher in His second coming. Many in this day and hour do not understand the importance of God's prophets and the role they will play in this great move of God. Prophets are the very mouthpiece of God and usher in (or speak forth) the move of God. Prophets sound alarms and shout from the housetops when God speaks. Every generation has seen a great move of God, but this current generation may very well see the greatest move ever upon the earth. God desires to speak and He is raising up true prophets in this hour that will do His will.

For every one true prophet there are many false ones. In the last days you will see many claiming to be prophets of God that will only come to kill, steal, and destroy. They will be false prophets who the enemy has raised up to speak deception to the church. It is more important than ever that the true prophets of God get in their positions as watchmen on the walls. How will the world be spared if someone is not watching and interceding? God is raising up the true prophets and the true watchmen of this hour.

Not everyone reading this book is called to the office of prophet. Anyone can prophesy, but only a few are selected as a prophet of God. Prophets carry mantles and authority that others can operate under. With this mantle and authority comes great responsibility. God will hold the prophet accountable for what they do and for what they don't do. Ezekiel 33:6 says, "But if the watchman see the sword come, and blow not the trumpet, and the people be not warned; if the sword come, and take *any* person from among them, he is taken away in his iniquity; but his blood will I require at the watchman's hand." Prophets are commissioned to be God's watchmen and are required to warn God's people. The cost of being a prophet of God is your life, your reputation, and every part of your being. All of this is in order to walk in the anointing and power that God is about to release. It will not be an easy walk, as it will be filled with tests, trials, and tribulations. You will learn things about yourself and others that you did not know as God examines your heart for the things that are not of Him. He will allow situations to happen in your life that will make you dependent on Him in order to make it through. He will teach you that when you trust and rely upon Him that He will always make a way for you and that all things are possible to all who believe the Word of the Lord. The Lord loves to create an intimate relationship with His prophets so that they will know and trust His voice. Prophets are designed by God to have fellowship with Him, to walk with Him, and to hear His voice.

As you hear His voice, you are called to speak the Word of the Lord to the people. God chose Moses, Elijah, Elisha, Jeremiah and many other men to be His prophets. As you read in the Bible about the Old Testament prophets you will see that their lives were not easy ones. They were faced with hard situations, traps, persecutions, enemies, lack, and even rejection. Many of you face some of these same challenges in your life. You mean well in your relationships, your jobs and your ministries, but somehow you seem to be always misunderstood, rejected and even overlooked. Many of you have seen where the enemy has even taken your substance and delayed your blessings. Nothing seems to work out for you, and you don't know why. It seems like you just don't fit into the church or the body of Christ. Everyone else could be praising God around you, but you may feel in the spirit that something is wrong and you will not be able to relate to what is going on around you. As a prophet of God, you are made up differently than people called to the other four offices. The way you think, the way you respond to God and the way you move with God will often be different than others around you. The real challenge for any prophet is to keep your sanity. The devil will attack the minds of the prophets and tell them that they are not accepted, not loved, a failure, crazy and rejected. Even though people in your life love you, they may not be able to communicate with you the same way you communicate. They may not understand why you can't just shake things off and move forward. Things you do, things you say and things you don't say can be misunderstood and cause you problems in your life and ministry. The reality is that a prophet's life is shaped over time. It can take years for someone to finally realize that they are called to be a prophet. It is often years later after failed situations, attacks, battles and war wounds that we finally understand that God has been preparing us for a greater work.

If you are called by God to be a prophet you may have some of these characteristics:

A. You have had a life that has been tried and tested with many battles and spiritual attacks. It seems that the attacks have happened for years and may never end.
B. God seems to be examining your heart all the time while others in the church don't seem to be held to the same standards by God. The Lord often holds prophets to higher standards of self-denial.
C. You have a gift of knowing what to pray. There will be an intercessory gift that the prophets will flow through.
D. There will be a strong desire to worship God. Prophets tend to be deeper worshippers and love worship. Often the prophetic gift moves more during worship.
E. There will be signs, gifts and wonders that follow a prophet's life. These may be physical, spiritual and even financial

miracles. These include gifts of healing, deliverance, and prophecy.

F. You will know things about circumstances, situations and people without anyone telling you. You could be just talking to someone and be prophesying and not know you are. The person may ask you how you knew what you just spoke.

G. You will often have a poor opinion about the state of the church. God will often show His heart to a prophet about a church or ministry. Prophets often feel like they are being critical about the church because God often reveals His heart through the prophet concerning the state of the Church.

H. You may prefer to be alone more than with others. Prophets often have a hard time relating to other people and will gravitate towards isolation or have few people who are close to them. Often others have a hard time being friends with prophets too, because they are so different.

I. You hear God speak and can prophesy to others. This may seem obvious but there are many that are so called prophets that cannot hear God and do not prophesy to others.

J. You have dreams and visions. Many prophets are dreamers and have dreams that God speaks through. Others have open visions.

K. You may have a burning bush experience. Many prophets have had a burning bush experience with the Lord. He has appeared to them and spoke to them.

If you are called to be a prophet you may have some of these weaknesses:

A. A man pleasing spirit. You seem to want to please others more than God.
B. Fear of man. Prophets often fear man and have to learn to fear God more than what man can do to them.
C. Difficulty trusting God. This is one of the top areas that God works on in our walk as a Prophet.
D. Weakness to women such as Jezebel. The flattery and control of the Jezebel spirit moves through others to control a prophet.
E. Depression and self-pity. Many prophets are depressed, lonely, and are in a place of self-pity.
F. Pride. Some prophets will have pride issues when they begin to take credit for God's miracles. People will end up following the person's gift instead of God.

If you are unsure if you are called to the office of prophet, I would recommend that you begin to pray and ask the Lord to reveal to you your gifts and callings. Begin a three day fast and ask the Lord to confirm if you are to be a prophet. It is God who personally calls and ordains a prophet. Through your seeking and persistence, the Lord will begin to reveal His will and purpose in your life. Ultimately it is the Lord who will reveal our purpose and destiny. We must seek the Lord for His revelation on our calling and ministry. As we seek Him, it will become clearer as to what the Lord is doing in our lives. Others will recognize our gifts and callings, which will make room for us in the Kingdom of God.

CHAPTER 2

The Refining Process

Every prophet must go through the refining process. Even Jesus went through this process when He asked the Lord to let the cup depart from Him before He was to be crucified. His request to God was, "Father, please let this cup depart from me; but if it will not, please let it be according to your will." That is the same petition that each prophet should have before the Lord. Our prayer should be that if He wants to spare us He can; but if not, we will serve Him anyway. Our obedience to Him is non-conditional. It is a choice, and we have to obey Him no matter what the cost even if it means we lay down our lives, agendas and comforts of life. We must drink the cup that God has ordained for each of us to drink in order to see the fulfillment of God's word on the earth. We don't get to choose what is in the cup that we drink. Instead, we drink whatever God puts in that cup, whether it is fame, fortune, hardship or affliction. In the process of drinking the cup, we must lay down our lives to the point of death. This process may be painful and time consuming, but it is necessary for our good.

As a prophet in training, you may feel like you are being stripped naked before all men. God will reveal issues of the heart, motives and agendas that you did not know you had. He may show you that you are weak in areas that you thought you were strong in. You may become discouraged and even depressed during this process. Many will not even complete the process and will simply abort the mission that God has given because of frustration and disappointment. Instead of accepting defeat, God's prophets have to learn to face their storms head on. If a prophet runs from the storms and tests that God is allowing, then he or she is only delaying what God will do in their life.

There are many times even in my own life where I would run from my problems instead of facing them, and this only delayed my ministry. If I had been obedient to press on and push through some of my past tests, I would have seen a breakthrough in my life and ministry sooner. Instead, I ended up going around the mountain many times before I realized the schemes and patterns of the enemy. I had repeated patterns of behavior and sin that would prevent me from going deeper in my ministry. Once I realized what the common themes and patterns were in my life, I was able to better learn from them. There have been times where I have been jealous of other Christians that didn't seem to require so many trials, tests and attacks. It seems that, as a prophet, I have had to deal with so much rejection, hatred, and persecution that at times I wondered why God would even use me.

People will make you feel unworthy or unwanted in ministry, but in the end the Lord will turn the bad to your good. God allows the enemy and even our friends to attack us in order to pull out of us any spirit that will prohibit us from fulfilling our prophetic mandate. This is necessary to deal with man-pleasing spirits, unbelief, and issues of our hearts. God will most definitely refine a prophet by fire. One day things can be going well, but the next day the enemy can start hitting you with attack after attack. The enemy knows your destiny and purpose. He knows more than we do about what God has planned for our lives.

Prophets often feel that God has abandoned them or left them alone. It seems we can always hear for someone else, but we struggle to hear for ourselves. There are long periods of times that prophets have to walk by faith and not by sight. It is during these times that God will refine us and make us the chosen vessels He meant for us to be.

The refining process is filled with tests and trials. Just the idea of going through another trial or test is enough to scare many of us away from what God is calling us to do. To make it through the refining process we have to allow our selves to go through the fire. The Bible teaches that the fire refines or purifies gold and silver. The fire burns away the chaff and impurities. All that is left to withstand the intense heat is the gold or the silver. Just as God purifies the gold and silver, He wants to purify us. Fire also represents judgment, and God often allows our works to go through the fire so only those things done with the right heart stand before God. If we would learn not to run from that fire but to submit to the will of God and stay put in the fire, God could do a new work in our lives.

One of the main things that I have learned about tests and trials is that they are for my good. As a prophet of God, I am often hardheaded and stubborn. A lot of times prophets don't take the time to listen to God. He is trying to slow us down long enough to speak to our lives. God is always speaking, but are we listening? It is often in the fire that we actually are able to hear God. It is in the fire that God burns away those things that prevent us from hearing Him. As you read this book, I challenge you to pray over your life and see those times where God has refined you with fire. After God was done, were you the same? I am here to tell you that the Lord will take us prophets through the fire in order to purify our hearts and minds. Our minds are carnal in nature and must be changed. If the Lord does not change our minds, we are not able to accomplish His will. The Bible says that we will do greater works than Jesus did, but our minds often prevent us from walking in this level of anointing. The refining process is the way to promotion. Surrender to His will and chastening, and you will begin to see the will of God manifested in your life.

Here are some of the fires that I have seen prophets walk through:

- Delay. God will allow the enemy to attack your life to delay the promises to teach you to push through your situation. It is a test to see how determined you really are to serve God even if you can't see the blessing yet.
- Rejection. Many Prophets will step out in their zeal to do what God has called them to do only to be denied or

rejected by other people. This is a refining process to get us not to please people but to be one that pleases God.

- Unforgiveness. Prophets are continually hurt by people and must guard their hearts against unforgiveness. A hidden root of unforgiveness will negatively impact a prophet's life and anointing.
- Loss. The enemy will attack you and try to steal, rob and destroy from you to get you to quit. God will allow this for seasons to show you that it is not what you have that matters but who you serve that matters.
- Confusion. The spirit of confusion will attack your mind and heart. You won't know who loves you or simply tolerates you. It will be hard to hear God for yourself. God allows this, as He is teaching you to walk by faith and not by sight.
- Financial Struggles. Job had and then he lost everything. Sometimes it will feel like you are taking one step forward and two steps back, but God does not want us to rely on money as our substance. Instead, we have to be like Elijah, realizing that God even feeds the birds of the air.
- Discouragement and Depression. Often God allows discouragement to see whose voice we will listen to. As Prophets we have to reject the voice of this world and hear God's voice in our situation.
- Fear. You will have to deal with your fears in order to fulfill your call as a prophet. Fear is the opposite of faith and will destroy your life and ministry.

- Sickness. Many prophets face very serious health challenges because the enemy wants to stop them from doing God's will.
- Gossip. Unfortunately, people in the church love to talk about other people and often prophets are the focus of that negative attention. You will be talked about and defamed if you are a prophet of God. It comes with the territory. I have even seen spirits of jealousy come on people towards prophets.

CHAPTER 3

Schemes and Strategies against Prophets

The enemy has a variety of schemes that he uses to attack God's prophets. The problem is that we often don't recognize his schemes until it is too late. Many prophets get chased into their caves because they were not ready for the attacks of the enemy. 1 Peter 5:8 says "Be sober, be vigilant; because your adversary the devil, as a roaring lion, walketh about, seeking whom he may devour." In my life, I have seen first-hand how sneaky the enemy can be. When things were quiet and going right, I often was caught with my guard down as the enemy would blindside me with his attacks. I have learned over the years that it is when all the storms of life have calmed and all is quiet that we should pray and be alert.

It is very similar to how natural storms work. In the eye of the storm there is a quietness that will lull people into believing the storm is over, if they are not prepared. The back-end of the storm is often the worst, so we must always be in prayer. The Bible says to pray without ceasing. What I believe that means is that we are always to be interceding and alert for what will come next. Truthfully, I have learned that prophets don't get much rest. It seems the enemy hates prophets and will do whatever he can to terrorize them. In the next several chapters we will discuss the schemes that the enemy uses to attack God's prophets. By understanding these schemes, we can better prepare for the tests and trials we will encounter.

As you read each chapter you will learn more and more about some of the schemes the enemy uses against prophetic people. Do not let the enemy isolate you or pull you away from the body of Christ. You are a part of the body and have a purpose to fulfill. You are the mouthpiece of God, and His desire is to sift you like wheat. There has been much intercession for you through the Holy Spirit who intercedes for you day and night. Continue to run the race and do not stop no matter what the enemy says or does.

CHAPTER 4

Rejection and Abandonment

Most of my childhood is a blur because of the years of abuse that I went through, both mentally and physically. I had a very abusive father who would beat me, yell and scream at me and call me names. As I grew up, I was a hurting young man and longed to run away from home. I suffered the cruelest rejection anyone could suffer by my own father. I remember one time that my mother told me that I should try to hug my dad and tell him that I love him. My dad was not the type of man that would hug you, so this was a frightening experience to me. I remember trying to go up and hug him and his face changed. He got angry and accused me of being a homosexual. That was so hurtful for a young boy who just wanted the love of his father. See, home life was very painful, so much so that I used to pray to die every night to escape the pain I was in.

School wasn't much better. I was one of the smallest kids in my class and not very popular with the other children. Because I had the last name "Bacon," you can imagine that I was picked on quite a bit. I was often taunted and teased by other kids. It seemed no one loved me and all I wanted was acceptance, but I couldn't get that at home or school. By the time I graduated high school I had no self-confidence. I had a very poor self-esteem and would constantly be intimidated by other people. I was literally afraid of people. I couldn't look anyone in the eyes or have a meaningful conversation. Instead, I would look at the ground when I talked, and I would constantly say I was sorry in the middle of a sentence. In my mind no one could ever love me, and I was not loveable.

Then after all those years of abuse, I found out at twenty-one years old that my father that raised me was not my biological dad. In fact, the Lord spoke to me personally and again through my brother that this was the truth. I went to my mother and asked her about it. When I told her what the Lord said, she broke down crying. She confessed that she had gotten pregnant unknowingly by a married man when she was very young. The man had deceived her, got her pregnant and left her to handle it all on her own. Apparently, he had done this to several other women in town as well. My mom did what she thought was best and accepted a proposal of marriage by a man she had previously dated prior to getting pregnant. I am sure to her this was a kind act from this man, and she most likely had no clue of what kind of person he would become or how he would treat her children. It was all a secret that was kept from me my entire childhood. I know my mother loved me and tried to protect me by not telling me, but this really hit me hard, especially after all the years of abuse and rejection from the father that raised me.

When I learned the truth, I had so many unanswered questions and a longing desire to meet my biological father, but I could not find him for many years. When I did find him later in life, he also rejected me and refused to meet me. He has many children from other marriages and children from outside of marriage that also refused to get to know me. I suffered rejection not only from the father that raised me but also from my biological father and half siblings. But like anything God has used that to my good. There is one half-brother that I am very close too, and it has become a blessing to my life.

What we go through in our childhood often affects us in our adult years. What happened to me when I grew up is what happens to most people who have been through mental or physical abuse. We do anything to get people to like us. It is called a "Man-Pleasing Spirit". The man-pleasing spirit will cause us to do things that are against our nature and against God's word. We compromise whom we are as a person just to fit in or to be accepted. We either deny our calling because others do not recognize it, or we simply bow down to other people's desires to avoid further rejection.

God never called us to please man. We were formed to please God the Father. He created us to please Him and to do His will on earth. Yet, many of us, because of our hurts and pain of the past, will go through life trying to find acceptance instead of being satisfied by God's love. That is why we often are easily hurt in ministry. We care too much about fitting in or earning another's approval.

Prophets must not be easily hurt or offended. We have to love much even when we don't feel loved. The Bible says that love covers a multitude of sins. As prophets we have to protect ourselves from offenses. If we are not careful to guard our hearts, then we will take the gift of prophecy and use it as a weapon through a critical spirit towards other people. I know it sounds unloving, but God has to break prophets who have suffered much rejection. Otherwise, they will see out of the eyes of rejection and not see the way God sees things. This can cause a prophet to prophesy out of a past hurt or the flesh instead out of the heart of God. I know that I have had to forgive family and friends who have rejected me. This has been a constant thing that the enemy has tried to put in my face, but I still choose to love them all even if I don't feel they love me.

Prophets also suffer from abandonment issues. I went through wanting to be accepted. I wanted to be a part of a group of people that loved me and cared about me. I didn't want to have to go through hard times in life by myself. Unfortunately, people will often abandon the prophet, because the Lord will cause them to separate. It is the Lord's doing, as His desire is for the prophet to walk through many things alone. Technically, the prophet is not alone and has God with them, but it feels like we are alone at times. We look for others to encourage us to only find out they have left us. Actually, this is all part of God's doing. Even in my own life, I have fantasized about what it would be like to be raised by my biological dad. I thought about how my life could have been different, but, in reality, it could have been worse and not better. Satan loves to play out "what-if" scenarios in our minds. It is better to just trust that God turns every bad thing to our good according to the Word of God.

Abandonment also extends into ministry, as many people will say they are for you and walk with you for a season; however, for whatever reason, they will no longer walk with you, as they are easily offended. I believe the Lord actually allows some people to become offended so that they will leave your life and, as a result, His will not be hindered in your life. I also believe the enemy uses that person's departure from your life as a weapon to tell you that there is something wrong with you. The truth is that every prophet is a work in progress. God is doing something good in our lives.

God has a plan and a purpose in the prophet's life and every life event contributes to that calling and purpose. We cannot spend our days wondering "what if", or fantasizing about what could have been. We have to allow God to heal us and do His will and purpose on the earth.

The Lord showed me that Jesus felt the same way many prophets do. He asked His disciples to stay up and pray with Him, but they were too tired. There will be days when you (as a prophet) will have to overcome rejection and abandonment and walk alone with God. It is in those seasons of walking alone that I have grown the most in the Lord. Yet, those were only for seasons, and God has a purpose for us in the body of Christ. Do not let the spirit of rejection be the tool that hardens your heart or chases you out of position.

CHAPTER 5

A Man-Pleasing Spirit

As mentioned in the last chapter, the man-pleasing spirit is a major assignment against the prophet. Many times, what the Lord will tell a prophet to do will contradict what other people would do. We cannot fear or worry about what people will think about us when we obey God. One of the major schemes of the enemy is to use people close to us to discourage or even stop us from fulfilling our destinies. We must love people, but we must obey God. If we listen too much to what people are saying and what their opinions are, we can often get off track from the will of God. It has been my experience that people we love can be the worst critics when they do not understand the plan of God for our lives. They can also give us wrong advice that can majorily delay the completion of God's work in our lives.

I am reminded of the story of Job when his friends and family told him to curse God. Job understood that he could not blame

God or get angry with God; because it was a test that God was allowing him to go through. Even Jesus went through a season where people became a limitation to Him. He was unable perform miracles in His hometown simply because they knew Him as a man. Your family knows your whole history. They know where you came from, all the mistakes you made when you were younger and even what you are going through right now; but they are unable to see what God sees in you. They are unable to see the destiny and the purpose that God has for your life. We cannot live our lives pleasing people or trying to make them understand where we are spiritually. Unless God opens their eyes, they will not be able to see it.

I have seen too often in church where pastors, leaders, and even the congregation can hold a person back from a powerful destiny with God, because they do not encourage their gifts or see what God is doing in them. God does not look at the outside, but He looks more upon the heart of the person.

If people could see what God sees in you, then it would be much easier to walk out the plan of God in your life. The truth is that normally people cannot see what God sees about us and therefore will often unknowingly or even intentionally try to stop us from going in a direction they do not understand. Often the person or person(s) believe that they are somehow protecting us and that we have lost our minds. I have to admit, at times, I have even thought I had lost my mind, because I could not understand the ways of the Lord. The enemy will discredit and even try to control us through others. He will get us so worried about being accepted that, if we are not careful, we will give up our destinies to become something we are not.

Early on in my life, and even into my adult life, I suffered rejection, criticism and even judgments from others. Until I learned the strategy of the enemy, I was always apologizing for things I didn't do or trying to make peace with people that were offended with me over nothing. I didn't realize that even the offenses people had against me were part of God's strategy for my life. I wasn't allowed to get close to everyone. Not everyone could understand me or where I was being called to go. One day the Lord spoke to me and told me these words: "Michael, why are you trying to make everyone like you? Why are you trying to take everyone with you? Michael, not everyone is called to be an eagle. Eagles fly at altitudes at which not everyone else can fly. A dove cannot fly as high as an eagle. Even a hawk cannot fly as high as an eagle. Michael, why are you trying to make a duck behave like an eagle? Son, not everyone is the same. They can't make you something that you are not, and you can't make them something they are not." When I got this revelation, I began to realize that people unknowingly were trying to control and manipulate me into being something other than what I was called to be. I came to the realization that I needed to be the eagle that God called me to be and not to worry what others thought about me.

Many do not understand how much time is wasted worrying about how others feel about us. It is not that we should not care, but we need to understand the strategy of the enemy. I cannot change whom I am or what I am called to be to make someone else feel comfortable. Many days I wished I could hide in the crowds and be liked by others. Yet, there are no substitutes for the love of God. When no one else is there for the prophet, God is always there waiting for our fellowship. You are not alone. You are with God.

CHAPTER 6

The Spirit of Fear

One of the reasons we don't see more signs, wonders and miracles is because of the spirit of fear. Fear is the opposite of faith. Faith believes the Word of God and what God says He will do. As a prophet, I speak faith or I speak unbelief. There is power in my mouth over life and death. I can either speak a miracle, or I can speak a curse. If I operate in faith, I can speak the impossible, and it will become a reality because in my heart I believe the word of God. Satan can try his best, but he cannot stop a prophet from moving in miracles, signs, and wonders. Only a prophet can stop himself/herself from moving in the power of God through their unbelief.

A prophet cannot have the spirit of fear. Fear is synonymous with unbelief. To have fear is to have unbelief. Satan uses the spirit of fear to stop the prophet from releasing the miracles. Depending on how you grew up, there are different tactics and strategies that the enemy can use to instill fear in the prophet. Fear is a learned behavior that is based on a life experience. There are several different types of fears that the enemy tries to use to control or limit the prophet:

- Fear of people. The enemy loves to use people to speak fear and unbelief into our lives. If we listen to what people say we will be full of fear. We should be encouraging people not speaking fear into their lives.
- Fear of failure. Satan loves to tell people that they will fail so that they never try to do anything for God. The fear of failure causes many people not to even step out in the work of God.
- Fear of missing it. In the prophetic office, the enemy will try to get us into fear saying that we are not hearing God or getting us to question whether the word is from the Lord. If we are not careful we will never open our mouths. It takes faith to prophesy.
- Fear of backlash. I have seen first-hand how the enemy tries to retaliate every time I serve God. Soon after serving Him an attack usually comes. The enemy has even tried to get me to stop ministering, trying to convince me that my life would be easier if I didn't. The reality is that he has no power over me. I can pray and stop his attacks.
- Fear of criticism or judgment. This is a big one. If you are called to be a prophet, many people are not going to agree with your ministry. They will call you a fake or false prophet. They will accuse you of things in ministry. You

cannot fear what they will say about you. If Jesus was talked about, you will be talked about

As a prophet of God, we must destroy the spirit of fear in all areas of our lives. Fear is made apparent in the circumstances we go through. If your first reaction is to fear or to operate in the spirit of fear, then you need to pray for freedom from that fear. One of the ways to defeat fear in our lives is to do what we think we can't do. I have to make myself step out sometimes to do things that seem impossible to remind myself of the Word of God. The Bible teaches that all things are possible through Christ Jesus. Make a list of the areas of your life where you live in fear. Then pray over those areas and ask the Lord to remove those fears from your life. Some of God's prophets may even need to be delivered from the spirit of fear in order to be used by Him. Fear is also an open door to the enemy in our lives. We must close the door of fear so that faith can grow within us.

CHAPTER 7

The Spirit of Pride

Pride is not a new scheme for the enemy. It was because of pride that Satan fell from Heaven. God did not tolerate the spirit of pride in Heaven, and He certainly does not tolerate it in the earth. The Bible clearly teaches that when a person enters into pride that it will lead to a great fall. There are many ministers who walk in pride and even fall into sexual or financial sin because of it.

I believe this was the case with Saul, too. Saul fell into sin, because he disobeyed God's word; but the core issue could have very well been pride-related. Many people do not listen to what God is commanding them to do, because they think they know better than God or somehow they think that if they do the thing God said not to do that there will be no consequences. Sin and pride go hand-in-hand and will result in our anointing being taken from us. Saul lost his anointing and position to David whom God raised up as a shepherd boy because of Saul's disobedience to the Lord.

I am seeing a trend today where people are chasing the title of "Prophet" so that others will idolize them. I have even heard prophets call themselves "Master" prophets and others "Minor" prophets to suggest that they are higher than another. The term Master implies that someone is your slave. In the kingdom of God, we are only slave to God not to man. There are more people today claiming to be prophets then I ever have seen in my lifetime. Why do so many have to be called by a title to be of worth to Jesus? It is such a major problem in the church. Some ministers will not even talk to you unless you address them by their title. I have never heard Jesus require anyone to call Him by His title. This was not a requirement, because He was servant to all. We are called to serve one another as Christ served the church.

The Bible also says that a man's gift will make room for him. Proverbs 18:16 says, "A man's gift makes room for him, and brings him before great men." My title is merely a representation of the function that I walk in. It is the gifts that I walk in that will tell people who I am and who I represent. This also supports the idea that we will know people by their fruits. Many people are calling themselves prophets but have no fruits of prophecy. I have been to numerous meetings and prophetic gatherings with these so-called prophets. The shame of it is that most of them can't even prophesy. They are called prophets but have no fruits of being a prophet. I remember once where Jesus saw a fig tree that bore no fruit and cursed it. We need to be careful today with claiming to be something we are not. We need to be even more careful to become puffed up, because so many people are following us as a person instead of following the God in us.

Saints, today many Christians can't hear God for themselves as they once could. Instead, they want to seek out a person that claims to be a prophet so that they can hear from God. Isn't this fortune-telling? As a prophet most of what we release to people should not be new revelation but should rather be confirmation of what God has already been telling them in secret. What I hear coming out of the pulpit these days is not prophecy but fortune-telling, telling the people what they want to hear to get money out of people or to make a name for themselves. It has become a form of idol worship in a lot of cases. Many Christians are going from meeting to meeting to worship the prophet.

The Bibles says there will be no other God before Him. We are to worship the living God. Prophets should never steal God's glory or take credit for what He is doing. The trap that the enemy is laying for many prophets is that they will quickly begin to take the credit for what God is doing in meetings. People will most certainly idolize them and even seek them out instead of praying to God for a word directly from Him.

There is so much of an abuse of prophecy in the church. It is no wonder why some denominations have rejected the gift and the office. Prophets have to be like David who knew the importance of guarding His heart from sin. In fact, many of David's prayers were that God would search His heart for anything wicked. Recently in my own life, the Lord took me through a season where I had to pray for God to show me things that were not of Him in my heart. The Lord had me pray through each thing He showed me and began to remove from my heart what did not belong. There are many prophets that are in a cave of denial and do not realize that they have become prideful and arrogant in the work of God. The Lord even showed me where that could happen to me if I was not careful. It has happened to many ministers, and I believe many of them started with the right hearts only to fall into pride, sin and error.

It will be important for each of us that are called to the office of prophet to have accountability to others and to continually seek our hearts to see if there is anything that is not like God. We need to stay in a place of humility and know that God can stop using us any time He chooses. Ask God to search your heart today and show you if there is any pride that you need to repent of in your life.

CHAPTER 8

The Spirit of Confusion

We read in 1 Corinthians 14:33, "For God is not the author of confusion, but of peace." One of Satan's primary weapons against the saints of God and His prophets is the spirit of confusion. Confusion is defined as the lack of understanding or certainty. It can also mean a situation of panic or a breakdown of order. We know that God is one that believes in and practices divine order. There is no confusion or chaos in Heaven. There is only order and peace. It is Satan who wishes to disrupt God's kingdom to cause confusion so that He can more easily attack the church. If the church does not have the understanding or certainty of God's divine intervention, it will certainly be caught off guard when the enemy attacks.

I have studied a lot about warfare and one thing that I know is that the enemy will often try to cause some type of confusion in our lives in order to catch us unaware. When God's people are sober and alert it is hard for the enemy to take new ground, but when they are in confusion and not operating in order it is very easy for the enemy to sneak in and destroy the church. Prophets are called to be watchmen on the wall: alert, ready and watchful of what is happening in the natural. Prophets are to look out for the sheep and ensure that the enemy will not destroy God's people. Watchmen are strategically placed in the kingdom of God to protect the saints. We know that any confusion in the camp can make it extremely easy for the enemy to invade the church. Confusion is nothing more than a tactical distraction so the enemy can attack and destroy the church. As leaders we should always be prayerful and watchful to pray against all confusion that may try to come into the body of Christ. We need to understand that the spirit of confusion also comes strongly against God's prophets. When we are in confusion, we cannot hear God's voice and we end up making bad decisions. Confusion causes us to act and behave differently than the Word of God requires us to. If we allow confusion to come, it will confuse us in such a way that we will miss what God is saying to us personally and corporately. It is imperative that every prophet stands still in any moment of confusion until they hear God speak. As the Lord told Elijah, "He is not in the wind or the rain, but He has a still small voice." God's voice is quiet and gentle, and, according to the Word of God, His sheep hear His voice and obey.

We cannot hear or obey if we allow the spirit of confusion in our lives and ministries. Whenever confusion comes to us it is simply Satan trying to stop us from being obedient to God. We need to understand this tactic and respond accordingly or we will lose days, weeks, months, and even years in confusion instead of accomplishing His will or purpose in our lives. One thing I have learned as a prophet of God is that we often have to do the opposite of what our flesh wants to do if we expect to please Him. This is not always easy, as our flesh loves to show itself in the wrong ways when confusion comes to us. We must defeat the spirit of confusion as quickly as it comes to us or we face major repercussions or delays to the will of God. In some cases, confusion may operate as an agent of death or destruction in the life of the believer. One failed assignment by the prophet can result in someone being doomed to hell or someone not receiving his or her healing or deliverance. If you are in a season of your life where there is confusion, I would ask you to step back, pray and ask God to restore His peace in your life. Command all confusion in your life to go so that you can hear the voice of God.

CHAPTER 9

The Critical Spirit

Too often I have seen hurt people trying to minister to hurt people. We cannot minister the love of God to other people when we are overly critical of others or walk in the spirit of judgment. As a prophet we sometimes get angry at people's sin just as Jonah did. We somehow think the worst about God's people when we should see what He sees about them. Unless we have the heart of the Father concerning others we should not be prophesying into their lives. There will be an hour where judgment will come to the church and to the world but God wishes that no person be condemned to hell. As a prophet you have to learn the love of the Father so that you can demonstrate that same love to others. If you have not been healed in your heart of the pain that you have, then you will minister out of the wrong spirit. This is something we see happening all the time with prophets.

The love of the Father is not part of our lives unless we have spent a considerable time in His presence to know Him. In His presence He will heal all of our hurts and pain. He will remove that critical spirit that wants to attack people versus building them up. No matter what office you walk in your desire should be to heal, restore, encourage and build up. It should never be to condemn, destroy or tear down. Even when God corrects us He does so out of love and concern for our souls. With the same level of love and forgiveness He has released into our lives, we need to release into others. God will often remove anything in a prophet's life that will cause them to minister out of anger, criticism or judgment. For as much as God forgives the prophet for his or her sin, so God wants to do for others. Sometimes we forget where we come from and God has to humble us and remind us of what He has done in our lives. We cannot look at the current state of a person and prophesy according to what we see or feel. We have to hear what God has for that person and only speak that which He instructs us to release. In the beginning years of my ministry, I had a lot of unresolved anger and ministered out of a critical spirit. Even though the words I had were from God, they did not bring life or revelation to people's lives. People felt condemned instead of being encouraged to change. Thankfully God delivered me of this critical spirit and gave me a heart of love to minister to His people. If you are battling this spirit, I encourage you to repent and ask God to remove it from your heart today.

CHAPTER 10

The Spirit of Control

Just because a prophet can hear from God does not give them the right to try to control a minister or a ministry. It also doesn't make a prophet closer to God just because they can hear Him speak. Often we see prophets trying to make the church something God does not desire. Prophets often bully and intimidate the pastor or the leader into doing what they think is right for the church. The problem is that the prophet is not a pastor and has no understanding what it means to shepherd a church. I know that before I became a pastor that I, myself, had some opinions of how a church should be run. I wrongfully felt that it was the pastors who were standing in the way of the Holy Spirit and restricting the flow within the services. I felt pastors were too controlling; and, therefore, I tried to force my views on the leadership to get them to change. This was not the right thing to do and was a form of control. At the time I justified it, because I felt God would want the Holy Spirit to flow in the church. Looking back on it I should have been praying and interceding and talking a lot less.

I have witnessed first-hand how prophets can destroy a church through the spirit of control. In fact, most prophets get angry when the pastors refuse to take their advice and begin to get people in the church to side with them. Because prophets can give encouraging words to people in the body, a lot of times they also have the power of influence and can sway people's opinions. If you are a prophet, the Lord will have to remove any form of control in your heart. He cannot have the prophets taking over the church or making their position higher than the rest of the five-fold ministry offices. Prophets are equal to the other offices, not superior to them. I think sometimes prophets feel they are on a higher level then the other offices and are not walking in the level of humility that they should.

CHAPTER 11

Speaking a Word out of Season

When younger prophets first begin prophesying they get very excited when they get a word from God and often want to blurt it out without God releasing them to do so. This is one of the biggest challenges when raising up prophets. I remember when I would get a word, and I would literally feel like I was pregnant with it during a church service. I felt I had to give this word or I was going to burst wide open. It was too heavy for me to carry the word, and the Holy Spirit would move on me so strong. Thank God that I had a good pastor who put protocol in place for young prophets so that no word was given to the body before it was judged. The pastor had people put in place so that, if any person got a word from the Lord, he/she would know what to do with it. Sometimes the word was for the body, and I felt so relieved when I was able to share it. Other times I was told the word was for myself or was something for me to pray about. Sometimes I would disagree with the person and feel I should give it any way, but I would, instead, listen to my authorities and not share unless I was asked to. While this may sound controlling, it was really a protection for me as I learned to flow in the prophetic. Just because you feel like you have a word from God does not mean you have to share it. Sometimes God is testing you to see if He can trust you with what He is showing you. Other times, He is teaching you to pray over the word, asking Him what He wants you to do with it. Whatever the case, prophets have to learn to flow the right way in corporate settings. You can have a true word from God; but, if you deliver it prematurely or incorrectly, it can really hurt someone. We have to learn to give words only when God releases us to do so. The timing can be critical for the person that is receiving the word.

CHAPTER 12

Offense

If there is any one area that I believe to be a stronghold in the church, it is in the area of offense. So many Christian believers claim to love God or to have a close relationship with Him, yet they are in constant offense towards believers and unbelievers. I have seen churches split over offense. The spirit of offense is so rampant in the church that Christianity has become a mockery of what Christ stands for. Christ is the fulfillment of selflessness and forgiveness. The church seems to have forgotten what Christ stood for when He was on the earth. He was the example of unconditional love and forgiveness. All mankind betrayed Him and allowed Him to die for sins He didn't even commit. Even His disciples, such as Peter, denied knowing Him to save their own life. Many people, who He had loved and poured Himself into, rejected Him. Even Judas turned His back on Christ and sold Him out for some pieces of silver. If Christ understood betrayal and offense, but yet freely forgave, how can we do any less than what He did?

Prophets are very prone to personal offense. We don't fit in with other people in the church. We are often the odd ball out. We want so close to be accepted and valued in the body of Christ; but often we are ridiculed, the center of gossip or misunderstood. We have the ability to hear God for others, but many times we don't hear for ourselves. We end up in strange situations or arguments that we didn't see coming. In fact, I believe that most prophets don't go looking for offenses or problems with people in the church. They just seem to happen naturally because of the office they walk in.

It also seems that pastors and prophets are always at odds with each other. I have seen prophets openly rebuke pastors, and I have seen pastors openly rebuke prophets. At times, it seems, they are at war in the church. Even though the word of God teaches that we need a five-fold ministry presence in the church, we see a spirit of competition. This is why we don't see the miracles, signs and wonders in the church that we are called to walk in. Offense has come in to rest right along side the spirit of competition. The enemy loves division, and he loves to isolate God's people from being in unity with the rest of the body of Christ. Offense is the arch weapon he uses to divide us from the people we need to walk with or from the work that we need to do.

According to the word of God, we are called to die daily; yet we see people's feelings ruling, instead of what the word of God tells us to do. Prophets must die daily to the spirit of offense, or they will never achieve the will of God for their lives. As prophets, we must learn to get along with the other four offices and not take their lack of understanding or lack of mutual respect as a personal attack against us. It seems in the kingdom of God we tend to shoot our own instead of helping each other. As a prophet, if you become offended, you become unusable until you deal with your offense. You will literally be in a holding pattern until you forgive the person you have an issue with. It is not only forgiveness that is required, but you must also be able to walk side-by-side with that person. Often, it is the pastor that the prophet is offended with and it may require putting personal feelings aside to accomplish the greater good of the Kingdom of God.

Some of you may even feel convicted, because you left the church you were a part of in the wrong way. In fact, God could call you back to that church because you were not released from being there. Forgive those that hurt you and go back to where God sent you. Only leave there if God has given you instructions to do so. If you are out of position, you can't be an effective prophet. Prophets are sent to strategic locations and to a particular people.

CHAPTER 13

Persecution

Christ said, "If they persecuted me, they will persecute you." Why is it a surprise to God's people when we are persecuted by the world? We shouldn't be surprised by persecution, but we should expect it to happen. It is a sign that we are doing the right thing for the kingdom of God, if the enemy uses people to persecute us. If we were not a threat to his kingdom, he wouldn't waste his efforts to attack us. Believe me when I say that Satan is focused on those that are a threat to his kingdom. The time is short and he has limited resources (only 1/3 of the angels) at his disposal.

If you are being persecuted, you should count it all joy. It means you are making an impact and helping accomplish the will of God on the earth. I have come to terms with the fact that I will be persecuted. Prophets and persecution go hand-in-hand. Most prophets suffer persecution and need to continually be on guard to ensure they are ready for when the persecution and attacks come.

The interesting thing about persecution is that it often comes when we are least expecting it or from sources that we didn't think it would come from. In fact, the enemy is gifted at turning Christians against Christians. I think sometimes it would be easier if all persecution came from outside the church, but the reality is that it comes a lot from within the church or from our own family or home. The people we think should be for us now suddenly turns against us for no apparent reason. All of a sudden, people we thought loved us are now accusing us of doing something we didn't do or questioning our motives even though our hearts are clean. This often occurs right after God uses us to do something in His kingdom. It is a form of retaliation the enemy uses to come against us as we are trying to gain momentum in the Kingdom of God. His goal is to get us angry, confused or in a place of stubborn retaliation.

We have to be a vessel that God will use to handle persecution in the right way. There is a right way and a wrong way to respond to persecution. How we respond to persecution will reveal the true heart that we operate in. If we are a child of Christ, then we can only respond with love or patience, which is opposite of what the old man would do in this situation. As the word of God states, we are a new creation in Christ Jesus. Our old man is now dead. All things are made new. Even our behavior and how we respond to persecution should change. Prior to Christ, we would operate in anger or revenge; but now that we are in Christ, we have to forgive as many times as necessary because we no longer represent us but Christ.

I am reminded of Jonah when he didn't feel the people of Nineveh deserved God's mercy due to their sins. He did not have the love of Christ or compassion that was necessary as a child of God. We will be persecuted, but we must respond out of the compassion and love of God even to the point where we want the best for that person. Of course, we know that the only way we can have the best is through Christ. The person persecuting you may very well be the one that Christ wants to win for Him through you. As a prophet of God, you must be ready for persecution. There will be seasons of persecution, and we must have the right heart and attitude when the attacks come. We can't target those that come against us or seek out revenge. Instead, we need to watch what we say about that person or how we react to their attacks. God is watching us, and it could be that we are simply being persecuted as part of a greater test. If you are facing persecution in your life, ask the Lord to give you the right heart and the strength to go through it.

CHAPTER 14

Self-pity and Depression

Have you ever noticed so many people in the church today suffering from self-pity and depression? It seems that this is a very common problem in the church. As a member of the church, the prophet often falls into this trap as well. It is so easy after long seasons of attacks, disappointments, tribulations, and persecution to suddenly feel depressed or to fall into a season of self-pity. We see many people dropping out of church due to these spirits. The person often feels alone and isolated and separates themselves from those that love them. The enemy is seizing the opportunity to convince the prophet that there is no hope for them and that no one can understand or help them. They become discouraged by what they see happening in their lives or their ministries. With no change or answer in sight, they begin to believe that their situation is the exception for God and that hope has run out. They begin to step back from serving

God or meditating on His word, and, instead, they entertain the lying spirits that speak to their minds on a regular basis. Even when brothers and sisters try to reach out to them to help, they can't believe that they are sincere or they believe that they have agendas. Having been convinced that God has forsaken them and that the church is part of the problem, they begin to hide in their homes choosing to alienate themselves from others. The enemy piles on the negative thoughts. Before long, the prophet is buried in a depression so deep that it would take an act of God to rescue them out of it. Their ministry is now stifled and ineffective because the spirits of self-pity and depression have taken its hold on them. People they once encouraged are now a distant memory.

Who are we to minister to anyone when God will not move in our own lives? See prophets can get resentful with God after a while because, they have seen so many lives changed and so many words come to pass for others, but their own lives are a ruin with no answers to their own problems. Many prophets question God as to why He can give them a word for other people but have no word for their own lives. Discouragement and even anger sets in, because we see so many other people getting set free and delivered yet we don't have what we are believing for.

I am reminded of Elijah when he sat under the juniper bush and said, "Woe is me". We have many prophets who have quit on God and are not doing His work in this hour, because they have a "woe-is-me" mentality. Just like Elijah, we get so depressed we would rather die than to have to face another day. It takes God removing the blinders on our minds before we can see the truth.

The first step in destroying the spirit of self-pity or depression in our lives is to ask God to show us the truth. The Bible says the truth will set us free. Many prophets have fled from the spirit of truth and have a chip on their shoulders because of lies the enemy has spoken to them. Why do we believe the father of lies? Shouldn't we, instead, embrace the spirit of truth? God wants to reveal truths; but, in order to find truth, you have to seek it. We have to come to the place where we realize that our minds can lie to us and convince us of things that are not real. Depression is like a disease of the mind. Once you suffer from depression you can no longer see things in your life as Christ sees them. If you are suffering from depression, ask the Lord to change your heart and mind so you can see your life the right way. God has good things in store for them that believe.

CHAPTER 15

Having an Unteachable Spirit

We have so many people wanting a title or a position but are not teachable. One of the prerequisites to being a leader is that you have to be able to follow someone else. Jesus was subject to His Father. John 5:19 says, "Then answered Jesus and said unto them, Verily, verily, I say unto you, The Son can do nothing of himself, but what he seeth the Father do: for what things soever he doeth, these also doeth the Son likewise." This implies that Jesus was always in fellowship with His Father, and He was only doing what He was instructed to do. Jesus also sent us "The Comforter, or The teacher" which is the Holy Spirit. In fact, He said it was necessary that He die that the Comforter comes to us. John 16:7 says, "Nevertheless I tell you the truth; It is expedient for you that I go away: for if I go not away, the Comforter will not come unto you; but if I depart, I will send Him unto you." This was an important statement, because He was telling us that we could not do the work and ministry of Jesus Christ without the Holy Spirit.

There are many in this hour trying to do His work in their own strength or in their own power; but, according to the Word of God, we must have the Holy Spirit. The Holy Spirit is to be our teacher, which means we have to be teachable. Those that have unteachable spirits are unworthy of ministry. Even His twelve disciples were under His teachings before He was crucified. Why do we see so many with the title of prophet who are completely unteachable? This is not only a problem with prophets but with all of the five-fold ministry offices. We have a lot of unteachable people in the church. It seems leaders think they are above reproach or already know what they need to know in order to effectively run the ministry, but this is nothing except a lie from the enemy. God is always teaching us new things and taking us to the next level of glory. There are many levels in God. The Bible says we are taken from one level of glory to another level of glory. There are so many levels in God, and each level is a new anointing or a new gift that God releases to His people. We cannot achieve the greatness of God or the miracles that He wants us to walk in, if we have an unteachable spirit.

I have learned the hard way that, when we think we have God figured out, He surprises us with revelations we had never seen before. If we remain teachable, He continues to teach us things that we wouldn't have been able to perceive in years past. There is a spiritual maturity that God wants to release to the church. Many prophets have left the church, because they couldn't be submissive or teachable under a pastor or leader in the church. This is error. We are technically called to be subject to one another. Even prophets are subject to prophets. Every prophecy has to be judged. We can't prophesy and not be accountable to anyone else. We must submit ourselves one to another. Even our words must be judged, and we have to be teachable when God wants to correct us. We are never too big in ministry, no matter who knows our names, to be corrected. God wants to teach us all the way until we are with Him in Heaven.

It seems that prophets have gone solo, having no need for accountability. If you have no one that you are accountable to, you run the risk of falling into error or sin. It is very wise to have at least one person you can be accountable to that can help keep you honest with yourself and God. As you read this book, pray and ask the Holy Spirit to give you a teachable spirit and a heart of accountability.

CHAPTER 16

The Spirit of Lust

As soon as I mention the word lust, our minds automatically jump to the desire for the opposite sex; but, in reality, lust is the desire for anything in the wrong way. That desire can be for power, money, position, sex or any other area of our life. What I have seen in the Kingdom of God is that many people who want to be in ministry have motives or hidden agendas that cause them to seek out a title or position. The Bible says that many are called, but few are chosen. I have meditated on that scripture, and I have concluded that God wishes for all of His people to be used in the kingdom of God. However, only a few people are qualified, because they have the right motives or right heart. When God sees His people, He can look right into their hearts and see the things that are not like Him. When we are seeking out a position for the wrong reasons, we are polluting His ministry and abusing His power for selfish gain.

The Lord is looking for clean vessels. We are to be vessels of honor that are qualified to carry His anointing. There is a qualification that is required to be worthy of carrying His anointing. When we have hidden lust issues in our heart, we are not qualified. In fact, the lust that we carry is enough to destroy the ministry or discredit His Name. We see so many church leaders committing adultery or stealing money from the church now. It is an issue that has brought embarrassment to the church. Many of these people were not chosen by God, but they were promoted prematurely by man because they were good speakers or they had a good personality. In reality, God chooses those that seem unlikely to us, such as in the case of David.

David did not look like a king. He did not have a muscular body, and he was not skilled at warfare, but God chose him because he was qualified. He possessed a humble spirit, holy life, and a teachable spirit. God tests those He has called, and we will be chosen based on whether we have passed or failed. These tests are things that we see every day. These are the hidden things that happen in our lives. What we do in private will determine what God will do openly. If we sin and compromise in secret for something we want, then we will do it publicly as His vessel. It begins with God dealing with us as His vessels to remove those secret lusts in our lives. Our only motive for being in ministry should be to please Him and to accomplish His will. It is not a way to get a paycheck or to get fame. Jesus has already told us that everything is His. Even the credit goes to God. He should get all the glory for the things happening in your ministry. It is not you who did it but the Christ in you. Check your heart today to see if you have any hidden agendas or motives for being in His ministry. If you have a love of money or lust for power, ask God to change your heart.

CHAPTER 17

The Love of Money

One of the biggest travesties that we see with prophets today is how they give words that people want to hear just to get a bigger offering or to ensure they are invited back. There is a reason God does not spell prophet as "p-r-o-f-i-t". If a man loves money more then he loves God, then he cannot be used by God to minister to others. Just like the Apostle Paul, prophets have to be content when they have things and content when they don't. I have seen prophets who have prophesied cars, houses, jobs, spouses, babies and wealth just to get bigger offerings. People get so excited to hear that good things are coming that they open their wallets and pocketbooks with bigger offerings. God will search a prophet's heart to see if they are money driven or God driven. He will remove the prophet's love of money.

Most prophets I know are not wealthy. I believe that is one of the ways God keeps them humble. At the same time, I do recognize that churches often take care of the pastor but fail to financially support the other four offices. We must remember that when we trust God He will provide and meet our needs. We cannot use our gifts or offices for drumming up more financial support. It is not wrong to ask for an offering, as we also see prophets such as Elijah ask for the widow's last meal; but we have to ensure that our hearts and motives are right. I believe it was the Lord who told Elijah to ask the woman for her last meal. I do not believe it was Elijah's intention to take from the woman of God but rather to see her blessed by God. When we have the right heart concerning money, we can be sure God will bless the people. He does not wish His people to be poor or to be begging bread. Often through the mouth of a prophet financial blessing can be released to the people.

CHAPTER 18

The Jezebel Spirit

Wherever you find a prophet of God, you will also see a Jezebel spirit; and wherever you find a Jezebel spirit, you will find an Ahab spirit. Jezebel used her weak husband to try to destroy all of God's prophets. In the end, we know that she was unsuccessful in her plan to kill all of God's prophets, but she did successfully come against and confuse God's prophet Elijah. Jezebel came after Elijah forcing him into fear, resulting in him running away from the work of God.

We focus a lot on what Jezebel did to the prophets of God, but what we rarely think about is that she was not the one who was supposed to have the power. In the natural King Ahab was supposed to be in power, and in the supernatural Elijah was supposed to be in power. However, Jezebel successfully took power from both Ahab and Elijah. She now was in control both physically and spiritually. In every church and ministry, the spirit of Jezebel is trying to seize control both in the natural and the supernatural. Church and governmental leaders have to be careful not to give their power over to Jezebel. Because of the power that Ahab had given his wife, there was nowhere for Elijah to hide. Instead of using His power to save the prophet, Ahab was surrendering his power to his wife to kill the prophet.

Elijah had given up his spiritual power too. He was now in fear over one woman who wanted to kill him. Where was the powerful prophet that had just been used by God to destroy three hundred prophets of Baal? Instead of destroying the Jezebel spirit, he was making it stronger by walking in fear and unbelief.

The spirit of Jezebel is a controlling spirit whose goal is to destroy God's prophets. Jezebel does not want the voice of God to be heard. She prefers that other gods are heard and worshipped. There are two types of Jezebel spirits: the high-profile Jezebel and the low-profile Jezebel. The high-profile Jezebel is very charismatic, outgoing and super spiritual. People immediately recognize her, because she is very determined to be heard in the church. The low-profile Jezebel is much more difficult to see coming, because she has a false sense of humility and is very quiet even operating in a shy or meek spirit. This is the spirit of deception at its worst, because often church leaders only recognize this spirit at the last second as she shows her true colors.

Any move of God in a church can be in jeopardy, if the spirit of Jezebel is not stopped from operating. God has placed prophets in the church to come against this spirit so that it does not destroy the church. Too many prophets are behaving just as Elijah did; and, instead of standing up to the Jezebel spirit and fighting against her, they are running and hiding in a cave somewhere. I have even seen this spirit in play in the local church. People are so terrified of a Jezebel spirit that they will leave the local church rather than have to deal with it. If you are battling a Jezebel spirit, you need to understand that it will move from person to person and location to location in order to get you out of the will of God. If you have encountered this spirit or allowed it to shut you down, then you should repent and get back into position.

CHAPTER 19

Witchcraft

Many prophets are unaware that there are many people practicing witchcraft today in the church. Prophets are often targeted by witchcraft, because the enemy does not want God's people encouraged or exhorted. Satan will use witchcraft in the church to shut the mouth of the prophet or discredit them. There are times that Christians unknowingly are practicing witchcraft. Witchcraft prayers are when a person prays out of the flesh or prays what they want for a person's life. We need to realize that God has very specific things that He wants prayed over His people. He has a will and purpose for every life. If we are not careful, we can pray things on people that God has not intended. This is often the case when people are praying for prophets. Christians will unknowingly be used by Satan to hinder the work of the prophet in the church. As a prophet, you will feel an oppressive spirit or something working against you, and you will not understand where it is coming from. If you feel this, you should pray and break every spirit of witchcraft in operation and break any curses so that you can be free to do God's work. I have learned as a prophet that I need to be prayed-up and sensitive to the Holy Spirit at all times. In fact, it is not just witchcraft prayers that Christians have to be concerned with. It is also witches who will target the prophet.

There have been times in my ministry where I have been heavily oppressed by witchcraft. The Lord has shown me that during these times there were witches and covens speaking curses upon my family and me. Because I am a busy man and focused on the work, a lot of times I do not always pick up on the attacks until they hit me in the face. Witches are very disciplined in how they curse people and will even astral project to leave their bodies to attack prophets. Witches are also very bold and will come into the church services under the disguise of a Christian just to hinder the prophet's flow. In charismatic and spirit filled churches, it is very easy for witches to hide. You would think that it would be hard with all the spiritual gifts in operation, but, frankly, it is easier than it should be.

Because of the years of attacks against me through witchcraft, I have put a few things in practice in my life to fight against it. First, as the Holy Spirit reminds me, I pray a prayer to break every prayer and curse put in the air against my family or me. I literally say I do not receive anything that has been prayed or spoken over me unless it is of the Lord. Additionally, before I preach or minister prophetically I bind every spirit of witchcraft in the service and close any open portals that the witches may have opened. This restricts the spirit of witchcraft from coming against me. I think sometimes prophets are too unaware of what is happening in the spiritual realm, and we need to see and warfare over that which would come against the meetings or us.

CHAPTER 20

Spiritual Backlash

If you are faithful to God and are used by Him, there will be retaliation from the enemy. Satan does not like it when we are obedient to God, and he especially doesn't like it when we take territories from him. When a prophet ministers to God's people, there are usually breakthroughs and transformations that come forth. Lives are often changed, and people start to press in more to God. The enemy literally hates it when God's people get new revelation that can change their lives.

The Bible says that the truth shall set us free. When God speaks through the prophet, there is a spiritual truth released that gives us the keys we need for victory and a breakthrough. The only way that the enemy can stop a move of God is to try to stop the vessels that God is using. Often he is unsuccessful in stopping the prophet from being used by God, so he will come after the meetings to attack them. Usually after ministry is over I am very tired because of how much God used me. I need a time of refreshing and a time for God to pour back into me. I am weak and tired after these meetings and even have to get rest. It is normally right after God does great things through me that the enemy will retaliate against me through some form of spiritual backlash. It will seem like all hell will break loose in my life. I will often be caught unaware or off guard with unexpected attacks. As a prophet, you need to understand how much the enemy is going to target you.

You will absolutely pay a price for the anointing that you walk in. However, the Lord has shown me that there are things we can do to come against the spirit of backlash. There are two things the Lord has me do after I minister. First, I break off any spirits that may have come or attached themselves to me after ministry. I also pray over those that pray with me the same protection. Second, I bind the spirits of backlash and retaliation that the enemy would send towards me. By doing this God moves to defeat Satan's attacks even before he can start them.

CHAPTER 21

The Cave Experience

In the natural, a cave is a dark damp place where there is virtually no life. Nothing can grow where there is no light. We know that caves were often used as a place to hide from bad weather or dangerous animals. We also know that they were used to dispose of dead bodies. Caves are very similar to tombs. The things that you find in them are often long forgotten, such as ancient paintings or old skeletons. Caves may be interesting to explore, because you don't know what you will find. Caves are not a nice place to live.

Elijah, who was crippled by fear and unbelief, was now hiding in a cave. When we read the Word of God, it seems that Elijah was in the cave because he was afraid of Jezebel coming to kill him. This seems to make sense, because Jezebel had killed several other prophets of God before Elijah had fled. On the other hand, it could be that there were other reasons that he now found himself in a cave. I believe that God uses everything in our life, including our mistakes, to prepare us for His work. We see in scripture that Elijah was asking God to take his life. In this case, could it be that God was bringing Elijah to the cave to have him die? The revelation here is not that Elijah would die physically but that he would die spiritually so that he could be used by God.

In order for God to use us, we have to be willing to die to ourselves. There are many prophets who are called by God that have fled to caves. They have left the corporate church and have refused to be part of a church family. They are no longer ministering the love of Christ to others due to self-pity and fear. They have hid, because the attacks on their lives have been too great and the price for the anointing too much for them to handle. Their fear and unbelief have rendered them useless and ineffective in the body of Christ, and they are now trapped in the cave due to their lack of faith. This cave represents the prison experience. Just like Elijah, many of us have thought that this cave was of our own doing, but in reality God led Elijah there, and He is leading us to the same place.

Let's use David's cave experience as an example. David was anointed as the new king of Israel, but he had a big problem. Saul was still alive, and he was the recognized King of Israel. Even though God had ordained and anointed David as king, he still had to wait patiently in a cave until his promotion. While fear of what Saul would do to him may have played a big part of why David fled to the cave, it was nevertheless a big part of God's plan to make him the future king. It was there that David died to himself and laid down any pride that he may have had. The time in the cave was not in vain; as God was not only preparing David, he was also preparing the world for David's unveiling as the new king of Israel. God was working the details out and preparing the way for his promotion.

The same was true for Elijah. Even though he was in a cave hiding from Jezebel, God was dealing with Elijah's heart and life while at the same time preparing him for victory in the natural. 1 Kings 19:13 says, "And it was *so*, when Elijah heard *it*, that he wrapped his face in his mantle, and went out, and stood in the entering in of the cave. And, behold, *there came* a voice unto him, and said, What doest thou here, Elijah?" Even in the cave, God was preparing Elijah's mantle and anointing. I believe that, by dying to himself in that cave, he gained a new level of anointing that would be needed to later destroy Jezebel.

There are so many prophets in the body of Christ that are in the same position right now. They are in a cave hiding from the many attacks that are coming against them. Instead of doing the will of God, they are running into hiding and have disappeared off the map. It seems like they will be lost forever, but, in reality, they have not been lost. They are in the process of transformation. Just as Christ was transformed from a mortal man to the Son of God in the tomb, so we are being transformed into His image into the mighty prophet of God. I know that the church and even many pastors have become frustrated with prophets, because it seems that they are running from the will of God, but we all know that you can't out-run God. He will find you and deal with you and get you back on the right road, especially when you have a call and purpose in the kingdom of God. We cannot out-run the hand of

God. We should be praying the prophets of God back into the local church. They do not belong outside the church. They are a part of the five-fold ministry. In order for the greater works to be seen, the true five-fold ministry must be restored. We need to pray that, while the prophets are in the caves hiding, there is death to the old man, healing and restoration into the body of Christ. The Lord has big plans for this hour and it involves the prophet walking before Him in obedience and humility.

CHAPTER 22

The Place of Brokenness

When we talk about brokenness what comes to your mind? Does it mean that we realize we have done wrong and now do right? Does it mean that we say we are sorry to the person we have offended? Does it mean that God crushes us or punishes us for our sins? No, what it really means is that we have reached the end of ourselves and now realize that without God we can't do it. We are nothing without God, and we need Him to even do the most basic of things in our life. True brokenness means that my flesh is now dead and that my will and emotions now belong to the Father. I no longer have feelings or emotions that control my life. It is no longer how I feel that matters. It is only to do the will of the Father in my life. My only purpose for living is to be His servant. I am not even worthy to tie His shoes or to sit at His table. Yet, because of His mercy and grace, I have the right to walk and talk with Him. God is so unbelievably merciful. He is patient and kind to us even before we are broken.

To come to a place of brokenness is not an easy task. It is a very painful process, because you have to let go of almost everything you hold dear to your heart. Not many people willingly lay down their lives for God. Most of the time God has to wrestle with us until we finally relax and give everything over to Him. As a prophet of God, this is often one of the biggest challenges you will face before you are qualified for ministry. Yes, I said qualified. When you are first saved and hear from the Lord that you are called into ministry, you may have felt that you were worthy of the call based on your salvation experience, but, in reality, you are not qualified for the call until you are broken. Just like a wild horse that was just caught, you are an unruly and undisciplined child of God. In order to become the fine stallion that can be used in the Kingdom of God, you have to be broken first. Man cannot ride a horse that is not broken. Man cannot use a horse that is not used to having a bridle. The bridle controls the horse to tell it what direction to go in and how fast to go. As a prophet of God, the Lord has to get you used to a bridle so that will you not only know which direction to go in, but also that you will only speak when He tells you to. Young prophets seem to open their mouths without thinking about the consequences. The longer you have been trained by God, the slower you are to speak about what you see unless you are sure God has spoken and told you that it is okay to speak the word.

One thing that I know from my experience as a prophet is that God does not always want us to speak. I also know that there are times that I think I know what I am doing that I really have no clue what I am doing. When I was younger in the Lord, I heard these words spoken to me, "When you first got called you thought you were qualified but you were unqualified. Later, after you were broken you thought you were unqualified, but it was then that I considered you qualified." When we are broken it does not feel good. We feel totally unqualified, but it is then that we are of use to God. He is the Potter, and we are the clay. He often has to break us down before He molds us into what we will be.

CHAPTER 23

Come Out of Your Cave

Part of the process of breaking us or bringing us out of the cave is to change our hearts. Unless we can see the things in our hearts that are contrary to His word, we cannot be broken or set free from our caves. One of the things I learned about David is that, not only was he a mighty man of God, but he also was forgiven for a lot of awful things he did in his life. I prayed one time and asked God how it was possible that a man that stole a man's wife and killed her husband would deserve such blessings in his life. The answer I received back amazed me, because I received a revelation from God. The revelation was simply that no man is good enough to deserve the blessing of God. God cares more about a man's heart than He does his actions, for the heart is where man devises evil and lives from. A man may do a bad deed but have a heart after God. I am not saying that the man has no evil in it, but the man is wise enough to pray and ask God to remove anything wicked from his heart.

I am often praying the same prayer that David prayed. I ask God to search my heart to see if there is any wicked thing; and, if there is, to remove that from my life. If you are to pray this type of prayer, you have to be prepared for the answer. God will indeed begin to show you the wickedness in your heart. He will show you if you really want to see. This is the beginning of your healing and deliverance of any cave in your life. It begins with God removing the blinders from your eyes so you can see yourself the way He sees you. We can deceive others in our lives and we can even deceive ourselves, but we cannot deceive God. He sees and knows all, even the things in our heart that we are unable to see or refuse to deal with. He wants us to pray that prayer and then to deal with what He shows us. Once you have seen, recognized and dealt with what He has shown you, it is now time to come back out of your cave. The death process has been completed and all issues of the heart dealt with. You are now able to come out of your circumstances and begin to do the will of God in your life again. For many of you reading this book, it is time for you to leave the cave that you have been calling home for so long. The Lord has need of you and it is time for you to move forward in what He has for you to do. Put your hurts and wounds aside and begin to do what God has called you to do.

CHAPTER 24

The Prophet's Great Commission

I pray that this book has helped you see that it is time to leave your cave and now begin again to do what God has called you to do. You cannot let fear or circumstances stop you from accomplishing the will of God in your life. This world needs more prophets that have been broken and prepared for this final hour. There is a great work that is to be done in this hour and you are called to help usher in the will of God. As the Bible teaches us, it is about fulfilling the Father's will by praying that what is in Heaven will now be released on the earth. There are many things about God's kingdom that we do not understand such as how God can love His people so unconditionally while they sin and continue to do evil on the earth. Yet in Heaven there is a great love that He has for His people that He wants released on the earth. This love covers a multitude of sins. His love is so deep and so wide that it could cover the earth many times over. No one can comprehend the love that God has for the people of the earth.

As a prophet of God, you are commissioned to be an instrument of His unconditional love and an ambassador of Heaven that encourages the brethren in this hour. God is commissioning the prophet in this hour to encourage and edify His children. We are to release what God has instructed us to say in this hour. Some of it may be basic words to repent of sin, but much of it will be words of encouragement for those that have grown weak or who are hurting in this hour. The Lord is truly speaking in this hour, and the obedience of the prophet to speak only what He says is critical to the end time move of God. The Lord has to be able to trust you with what He is saying in this hour, because He has a lot to say to the church that they may not be ready to hear. Time is short and it is very important that, as a prophet, you are in position to move when God speaks it. I pray as you have read this book that you will take the steps necessary to not only leave the cave you may have been in but that you will begin to advance the Kingdom of God wherever you go. Don't waste any more time fighting the schemes of the enemy. It is time to get up and to leave the cave that you have been hiding in. Go back to the local church, and begin to fulfill the call and destiny in your life. If you stopped prophesying, go back and prophesy again. Don't let religion or the enemy shut your gift down. Don't let the spirit of Jezebel or the spirit of fear stop you from doing what God has called you to do. Time is too short. It is time to rise up so that we can help usher in a great move of God. I challenge you as a prophet of God to stand up and get back to doing what God has called you to do. Don't let anything stop you because God has destined you for great things.

I pray you were touched by this book and that you will reach out if you would like to learn more. Look out for my future book on bringing order to the church in the area of prophecy. Blessings to you. Apostle Michael Bacon.

Made in the USA
Columbia, SC
06 May 2025